A Book
of Blessings
for Working
Mothers

A Book of Blessings for Working Mothers

ISABEL ANDÉRS

LIGUORI PUBLICATIONS

ONE LIGUORI DRIVE
LIGUORI, MO 63057-9999
(314) 464-2500

Copyright © 1994, Isabel Anders
Printed in the United States of America
First Printing

ISBN 0-89243-675-1
Library of Congress Catalog Card Number: 94-76024

Scripture verses are taken from *The Living Bible*
© 1971. Used by permission of Tyndale House
Publishers, Wheaton, IL 60189. All rights reserved.

Cover and interior art by Mary Thelen

ISABEL ANDERS is the author of a number of books, including *Awaiting the Child: An Advent Journal, The Faces of Friendship, The Lord's Prayer, Walking With the Shepherd,* and *Standing on High Places: The Story of Hannah Hurnard.*

A working mother for more than ten years, she is currently managing editor for Synthesis Publications. She lives with her family outside Chattanooga, Tennessee.

A WISE WOMAN
builds her house,

while a foolish woman
tears hers down
by her own
efforts.

(Proverbs 14:1)

I wish you the blessing of...

Mornings filled with sunshine and birdsong—

Enough light and sound
to wake everyone
in the family without
the harshness
of an alarm clock.

May morning beauty
catch them unaware,
and let the smiles of their
dreams stay on their faces!

She gets
up before
dawn....

(Proverbs
31:15)

I wish you the blessing of...

Looooong loaves
   of soft, fresh bread,
right within reach,
   that will stretch to make
every lunch needed.

Allow for many rounds of breakfast toast, and leave two pieces for yourself!

...to prepare breakfast for her household....(v. 15)

And, as well the blessing of...

Remarkably smooth traffic that flows like the workings of a fine Swiss watch...

All the way
to your favorite
empty parking spot!

She goes out to inspect
a field, and buys it....

(v. 16)

At work,
the blessing of...

Coffee breaks that creep up on you like surprise packages

you had totally forgotten—
    hidden in back closets
and pulled out for
    an impromptu party.

Times that
invite you
to rest your mind,
put up your feet,
and lighten
your spirit—

Leaving you refreshed
and ready for
whatever comes next.

She is
energetic,
a hard worker....

(v. 17)

Always, to you,
this blessing...

At the end of the day,
may you leave

the tools of your trade
behind—

Perhaps carry an empty briefcase, light as a feather,

held by one finger,
never touched,
never opened—

Throughout
  a relaxing evening
    of work-free,
    telephone-free
    hours.

...she plans
the day's
work....

(v. 15)

At home,
I wish you,
this blessing of...

A refrigerator that yields all the ingredients for the evening's meal;

No stolen bites
out of the dessert
you set aside
just to share tonight
with those you love;

And extra hands
to help set the table,
clear the plates,
and wash up too—
without leaving
all the work for you.

She is a woman of strength and dignity....When she speaks, her words are wise, and kindness is the rule for everything she says. She watches carefully all that goes on throughout her household....

(vv. 25-27)

But most of all,
this blessing of...

Voices that say,
   "I love you, Mom!"
and "You're the greatest,
   you know!"

With faces that
match the words,
plus hearts
that glow.

*Her children stand
and bless her....
"There are many
fine women
in the world,
but you are the
best of them all!"*
(vv. 28-29)

May all your working, loving life be filled with kisses and hugs and the closeness of kin;

With all these things
to make your hours golden

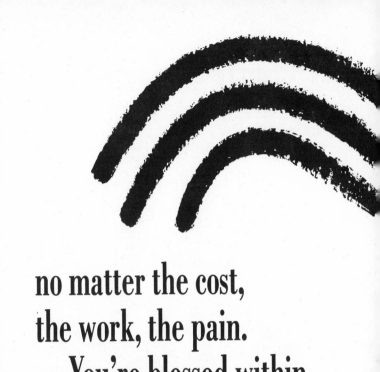

no matter the cost,
the work, the pain.
You're blessed within.

Charm can be deceptive
and beauty doesn't last,
but a woman who fears
and reverences God
shall be greatly praised
(v. 30).